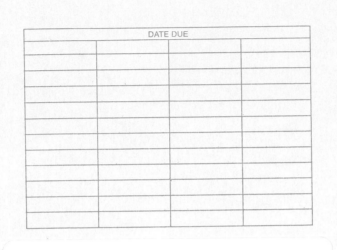

DATE DUE

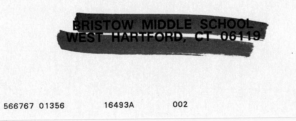

Jeremy Schmidt · Ted Wood

Two Lands, One Heart

AN AMERICAN BOY'S JOURNEY
TO HIS MOTHER'S VIETNAM

Photographs by Ted Wood

WALKER AND COMPANY ✹ NEW YORK

First published in the United States of America in 1995
by Walker Publishing Company, Inc.

Published simultaneously in Canada by Thomas Allen & Son
Canada, Limited, Markham, Ontario

Library of Congress Cataloging-in-Publication Data
Schmidt, Jeremy, 1949–
      Two lands, one heart : an American boy's journey to his mother's
   Vietnam / Jeremy Schmidt and Ted Wood ; photographs by Ted Wood.
          p.   cm.
      ISBN 0-8027-8357-0. —ISBN 0-8027-8358-9 (reinf.)
      1. Vietnam—Description and travel.   2. Sharp, Timothy James—
   Journeys—Vietnam.   I. Wood, Ted.   II. Title.
   DS556.39.S36   1995
   915.9704′44—dc20   94-33648
                                                          CIP

Book design by Victoria Hartman

Printed in Hong Kong

10   9   8   7   6   5   4   3   2   1

Contents

Heather (Phit), Jenny (Nga), and Jason (Khoa),
along with another foster child, soon after they
arrived in the United States.

Heather, Jenny, and Jason and their new
brothers and sisters. Bottom left to right: Jenny,
Jason, Jana, Joy. Top left to right: Heather, Jon,
Jeff, Jerry.

Introduction

It was as if the world had suddenly gone crazy, swallowing ten-year-old Phit and her younger brother and sister. Thousands of people filled the streets of Phit's small Vietnamese town in a panicked flight from enemy soldiers coming from the north. Helicopters beat the air around her, and mothers screamed in terror the names of their children lost in the sea of people.

Phit, too, had lost her parents, but she was afraid to move. The last thing her father said as he dropped them on the roadside was to stay put. He'd be right back with the rest of the family on his small scooter. Phit was too young to understand the war, but she saw the fear in her father's face as he sped off, leaving her to watch over her brother, Khoa, and sister Nga.

The year was 1975, and the long Vietnam War was almost over. The north was winning. Its army had launched a final push toward Saigon, the capital of South Vietnam. Caught in the path of a fast-moving battle, Phit's father was trying to move the family south to Saigon—to safety.

But he never returned. The flood of terrified people grew until Phit, Khoa, and Nga could no longer wait; they were swept up in the human wave. The three kids were pushed south through the mountains. Fighting and confusion swirled around them, and

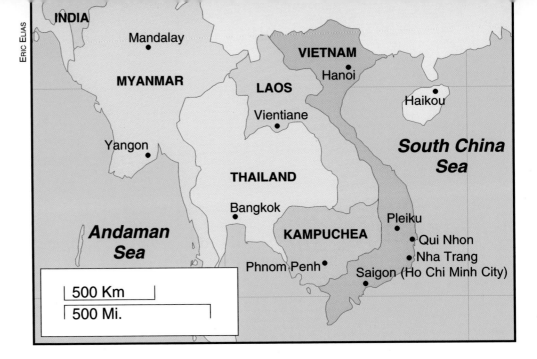

many children were killed. But Phit and her brother and sister were lucky. After two terrifying weeks they reached Saigon, where a priest took them to an orphanage for Vietnamese children.

Now safe, Phit waited for her parents to find them. But as the North Vietnamese Army closed in on Saigon, people became desperate, scrambling to find ways to escape. Then Phit's little sister Nga became very sick. With Saigon falling apart, the only help was in America, where war orphans were being flown for care. Phit had to make a hard decision: either send Nga alone for medical attention or have all three children go together. She had no way to contact her parents, no way to ask them what she should do or to tell them where they were going. But her father had said "Stay together," and that's what she decided to do.

Even going to America together didn't guarantee they'd stay together, however. One family would have to adopt them all, and luckily, the Shrader family of Colorado did just that. Jean and Frank Shrader became their American parents; the other Shrader children became their new brothers and sisters. The three were allowed to choose new American names: Phit chose "Heather," Khoa, "Jason," and Nga became "Jenny."

Heather, Jason, and Jenny grew up like any other American kids, with American names, attending American schools, playing American sports, and speaking English. Yet Heather never forgot where she came from. She worried about her Vietnamese parents, especially after she had children of her own and understood how terrible it would feel to lose your children in a war and never know if they were alive or dead. She was determined to find her family, if they were still alive. She wanted to see them again and let them know she was healthy and happy.

It took years of trying. In 1990, she made her first trip back to Vietnam, passing out pictures of her family and asking if anyone knew where to find them. But nothing turned up until more than a year later, when the letter she had hoped for arrived. An old family friend had found her family. They were all alive! Her mother, her father, three sisters, and two new brothers whom Heather had never seen had all moved to the family farm, where they had lived ever since the war.

As soon as she could, Heather—with her husband, Tim Sharp, and her brother Jason—made the journey back to her childhood home. The reunion was more than Heather could have imagined. Seventeen years of suffering poured from her parents the moment they saw Heather and Jason. The sadness of their long separation gave way to tears of joy. The family was whole again. But Heather couldn't stay; she had three sons of her own to take care of. When she left, she promised to come again, bringing her oldest son.

Seven-year-old Timothy James, or TJ, couldn't wait to go. He had seen all the pictures, heard all the stories. He wanted to meet his Vietnamese grandparents and all his aunts, cousins, and new uncles Thao and Truong, who lived across the Pacific Ocean. In 1994 his chance came. With his mother, his aunt Jenny, and their American mother, Jean Shrader, TJ set out on the biggest adventure of his life.

1 ➠

Flying to Vietnam

On the day of the trip, TJ is too excited to hold still. He tosses a football with his dad in front of their house and has a last-minute water fight with his brothers, whom he won't see for a while. He knows he'll miss them, but he can't stop to think about that now. The only man in the family going this time is TJ, and he

Left: TJ can't believe how far it is to Vietnam. As he and his brother Tyler look on, TJ's father maps out the long journey ahead of him.

Facing page: The day before his big trip, TJ has one last football toss with his father. TJ's dad is staying behind to look after TJ's younger brothers.

First page of TJ's scrapbook—the day they leave Denver.

has a special reason to feel proud. In Vietnamese families, his mother tells him, the first son is called the ''number one'' son, expected to be future leader of his family. It will be a great honor, she says, for her Vietnamese relatives to meet her number one son.

Aunt Jenny and Grandma Shrader meet them at the airport. TJ can only wonder about the long jet ride, which will take them halfway around the world, 10,000 miles across the Pacific Ocean. First, they fly to Los Angeles, where they board the huge 747 jet that will take them to Vietnam. It's two o'clock in the morning, and TJ can barely keep his eyes open. But walking onto the plane, he's amazed by how big it is. He can't see from one end to the other; it's like a flying town. Yet for all its size, a 747 carrying more than 350 passengers and their luggage doesn't have any room to spare. For once, TJ is happy he's small. He easily curls up in the airplane seat, puts his head in Grandma Shrader's lap, and falls asleep.

Meanwhile, thousands of miles pass beneath him. By the time the trip is over, TJ will have walked through five airports, ridden on three different planes, eaten five airplane meals (plus snacks),

Second page of TJ's scrapbook—the long flight to Saigon.

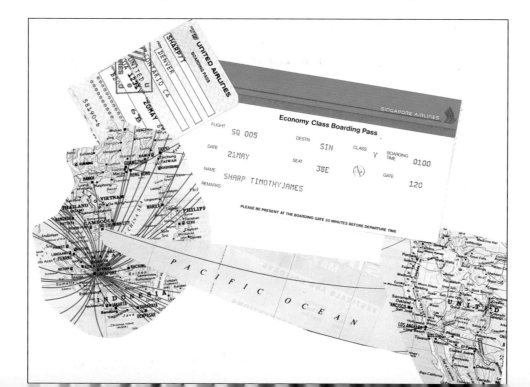

TJ treats his mother and her luggage to a fast ride though the Singapore airport.

and watched too many videos—more than his mom would ever let him watch at home. The thirty-hour trip feels as if it will never end, but finally Grandma Shrader, sitting beside TJ, points out the window. Below the plane, bordered by blue ocean, is the coastline of Vietnam. His first glimpse is of a green, green land. Everything is green except for slow, brown rivers winding toward the sea.

With a roar of engine noise, the plane lands in Vietnam. When it stops in front of the terminal, the flight attendant swings open the heavy door, letting in a blast of hot, humid air. Stepping outside feels like being dropped into a bowl of warm soup. TJ's skin is instantly soaked with sweat. The sun is high in the sky, but in Colorado it's the middle of the night. Back home, his father and brothers are fast asleep. No wonder TJ feels as though he's

As the jet passes over Vietnam, TJ and his grandmother Jean get their first look at the lush green land below (right).

The long flight to Vietnam.

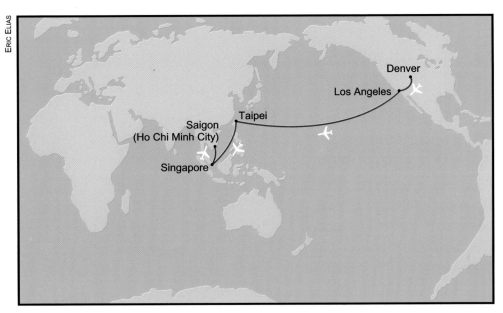

Eric Elias

TJ can't keep his eyes open any longer, so he sneaks a catnap on the Saigon airport floor while his family goes through the long customs process.

sleepwalking. It takes so long for his mother to fill out the forms, for customs officials to check their luggage, and for immigration officials to stamp their passports, that TJ falls asleep right on the floor of the terminal using his suitcase as a pillow.

At last his mom wakes him up, and they walk out into the bright sunlight. There, behind a tall steel fence, stand TJ's Vietnamese uncles Thao and Canh, waving bouquets of flowers. They've traveled two days from the family farm to the airport and they are so excited to see TJ and the family, they don't even wait to go around the fence. They hug each other through the bars, everyone crying but especially Jenny and Thao, a brother and sister seeing each other for the first time. Thao looks so much like TJ's Uncle Jason that it's hard to believe he's really a different person. When they finally go around the end of the fence, Thao takes TJ in a strong, welcoming grip and guides him safely through the crowd to a hired van. With the luggage loaded, they set off through the busy streets of Ho Chi Minh City, or, as the local people still call it, Saigon.

In spite of wanting to get to know his newfound uncles, TJ can think only of getting to the hotel and a nice soft bed. He falls asleep as soon as his head hits the pillow.

TJ's uncle Thao drove for two days from the farm to meet them at the airport. TJ watches as Thao and Jenny hug for the first time.

Vietnam is a hot country, buzzing with mosquitoes, so TJ sleeps surrounded by a bug net, common in all hotel rooms.

2 ➤

Chopsticks and Cyclos

*T*J wakes up starving. But he won't get eggs or cereal here. The usual Vietnamese breakfast is a bowl of noodle soup. TJ is willing to try it, but how can you eat soup with chopsticks? Uncle Thao shows him that the sticks are for the noodles. You slurp the broth straight from the bowl, something he could never do at home. On the table is more fruit than TJ has ever seen, and some kinds he doesn't even know how to eat.

Eating in another country is always an adventure, especially when there aren't any spoons or forks. But that doesn't stop TJ, who tackles a bowl of soup with chopsticks.

TJ takes his first ride in a cyclo, the bicycle taxi used in Saigon.

Saigon is a city jammed with scooters and bicycles instead of cars. At times the scooter traffic is so thick pedestrians can't cross the street.

After breakfast, TJ's mother wants to go to the open-air market, where everything from fruit to live animals is sold. To get there, they climb on bicycle taxis called cyclos. TJ has never seen anything like the streets of Saigon. Instead of cars, as in Denver, thousands of bikes and scooters flow by in one big, noisy river, so close that TJ can touch them. TJ feels like a small bug floating down this current as they pedal to the market.

If the Saigon streets looked busy, the market is a riot. Strange smells, sounds, and colors surround TJ. Everything you'd find in a supermarket—and more—fills the streets and alleys. A woman

The dragon fruit is particularly strange looking—and great tasting too.

The Saigon market seems more like a zoo than a grocery store to TJ. Animals of all kinds are sold, including ducks and chickens.

offers TJ some cloth, gesturing that she can sew some pants for him. Another has buckets and shovels for sale, a mini–hardware store right on the side of the street. The next woman is almost buried in a flock of ducks and chickens all quacking and squawking, waiting for someone to buy them and take them home for dinner. TJ watches as the buyer of a huge pig pushes it into a long, narrow basket and loads it onto a bicycle for the trip home.

Even the fruit is wonderfully different. The oranges are green. The papayas are as big as footballs. There are mangoes and pineapples, and about ten different kinds of bananas. But that's only the beginning. "Look at this," says Aunt Jenny, holding up a little round green thing covered with arms like octopus tentacles. It sure doesn't seem to be something you'd want to eat, but when she peels off the strange skin, the inside is like a white grape with a

TJ has never seen some of the fruits and vegetables for sale at the market. The baskets of colorful food seem to stretch forever.

TJ descends into one of the tunnels at Cu Chi, a
network of underground passages running for
160 miles beneath the rice fields and forests near
Saigon.

The Vietcong soldiers who fought the Americans and South Vietnamese hid and lived in the Cu Chi tunnels. They surfaced through secret trapdoors, fought, and disappeared again underground.

big brown seed in the middle. "It's like eating eyeballs," jokes TJ, but they taste good and he eats the litchi fruit as fast as he can peel them.

That afternoon, they make a trip to the tunnels of Cu Chi, a national historic monument in memory of the Vietnam War. The tunnels, stretching for 160 miles beneath the countryside around Saigon, were dug by Vietcong soldiers fighting the American and South Vietnamese armies. The Vietcong would come out at night through hidden trapdoors and go back underground each morning to hide. The opposing army could never figure out where they came from and were often caught by surprise. The tunnels are small, just the right size for a boy like TJ. They run in all directions through underground sleeping rooms and kitchens; it's the sort of place where TJ and his friends might like playing hide-and-seek. But then the guide tells about the war, when bombs shook the ground. He points out the hidden trapdoors and sharpened bamboo stakes designed to kill enemy soldiers. In the end, TJ decides there is nothing fun about the tunnels. These dark, cramped dens are the only place in Vietnam where he will see evidence of the war that tore this country apart and sent his mother to America.

3 ➤

Grandfather's Farm

TJ begins his journey from Saigon to the family farm, a two-day van ride up the coastal highway.

After two days in Saigon, it's time for TJ and his family to journey to the family farm. At seven in the morning, a chartered van picks them up at the hotel, and an hour later the city lies behind them. The brilliant green landscape of rice paddies, coconut palms, and tall clumps of bamboo looks like the country TJ has seen in pictures. But even out here, the road is busy with bicycles, scooters, horse-wagons, cars, trucks, and heavy carts pulled by water buffalo—the traditional tractors of Vietnam. With over seventy million people in this small country, the roads are always crowded.

Around noon, they stop in a small town for lunch. This restaurant seems just like an American one with tables and waiters and glasses of water. But what a menu! Grilled sparrows, eel soup, fried frog legs, snake-head wine, bird's nest soup. Maybe if his brother Bradley were here, TJ would order him an eel just to see if he would eat it. But for himself, he orders something familiar— fried chicken.

Then it's back on the road, which soon begins to climb into the mountains bordering the sea. TJ has never seen the ocean, and as the van tops the last ridge he spots the clear, blue South China Sea stretching forever before him. All he can think of is jumping into

The countryside along the coast is bright green with rice fields that spread as far as the eye can see.

Even in Vietnam kids make sand castles.
But TJ has never seen one anywhere, since
this is his first day ever at the beach.

that big blue pool, but he has to wait until they stop in Nha Trang that evening, where a sandy beach stretches for miles in front of their hotel. When he finally hits the beach, TJ can't believe his eyes. The beach is swarming with thousands of kids about his age. They try to play and talk with him, but TJ doesn't understand their language, and they walk away confused by his silence. Finally, he wades into the warm, gentle water and giggles as he bobs up and down. He wants to stay forever, but in the end, his mother drags him back to their hotel room.

TJ lives in the Rocky Mountains, and he has never seen the ocean before. Playing with his mother on the beach, TJ delights in his first feel of warm saltwater.

Small villages dot the Vietnam coast, and colorful fishing boats fill the calm bays.

Fishermen paddle these strange basket boats from the shore to their boats and back.

TJ can barely control his excitement as the van nears the family farm.

The next day they start early. It's still a long drive to the farm. The mountains are steeper now, and looking down, TJ can see fishing villages in sandy coves hundreds of feet below. As the afternoon heats up and they leave the mountains, the landscape begins to blur into sameness until the driver slows and turns off the highway. Pavement is left behind as they enter a shady tunnel on a narrow red-dirt road that winds between rice fields. Suddenly everyone is awake, both eager and nervous. After six days of traveling, they are moments from the farm.

The house stands back from the road, barely visible behind a dense stand of trees and bamboo. The driver honks the horn. Led by TJ's grandparents, a crowd of people runs out to greet them. They are weeping hysterically as they overwhelm Jenny and Heather. TJ is swallowed by a mass of arms touching and pulling him close. He doesn't know what to do. The crying and commo-

TJ, his grandmother, his aunt Jenny, and his many cousins crowd around the dinner table.

tion scare him, but he sees the love streaming from his grand-parents' faces with their tears.

With his arms wrapped around Heather and Jenny, TJ's grand-father leads the way back to the house. Set beneath big shade trees, the house is made of brick with a tile roof. The family crowds into a small dining room to talk over some cool coconut juice.

Although TJ already knows how to say "grandfather" *(nog)* in Vietnamese, all the talk is through an interpreter. After twenty years of living in America and speaking English, his mother has forgotten her Vietnamese. TJ would like to learn a few words, but

TJ is overwhelmed by his grandparents' tears of joy as they greet one another at the farm.

it's a hard language to pronounce. For instance, the word *dau*: If you pronounce it with an upward tone, like asking a question *(dau?)*, it means "headache." If you say it with a downward tone, it means "peanut." TJ might ask for a bowl of headaches, and what would that get him?

The next day relatives and friends come from miles around for a family feast. It's like a big Thanksgiving dinner with dozens of relatives crammed into one house. Even with tables in every room, people have to take turns eating. The American visitors are the main attraction. So many people are looking at them through the windows and doors that TJ can't see outside. From the kitchen comes an endless parade of dishes, some of them very weird to TJ. Who would think of putting spicy meat with fruit? Or of dipping sugary rice cakes in salty hot sauce? Or of frying a salad?

TJ likes some of the food, especially the fried rice. "*Nog!* Watch this," he says, and expertly lifts rice from his bowl with chopsticks. TJ wishes he could talk Vietnamese with his grandfather, but he's

TJ's grandparents throw a traditional feast to welcome them to Vietnam, with dozens of dishes TJ has never eaten before.

proud to show him that he can at least eat like a Vietnamese boy.

When he finishes, TJ wanders toward the kitchen. Of all the rooms, this one is the most different from houses in America. The only furniture is a table. TJ's aunts cook on the dirt floor in fireplaces with no chimneys, and the walls are black from the wood smoke that hangs in the air. Big kettles of soup bubble beside sizzling woks. There is no microwave oven, no electric stove, no blenders or mixers, not even a refrigerator. It's amazing to see a kitchen without any modern tools, but TJ loves it. It reminds him of his family camping trips in the Rockies. He takes charge of feeding sticks into the fireplace while the women of the family sit on the floor chopping and slicing.

Out the side door is the washing area. Instead of a sink there are several huge clay pots filled with water. The water comes from a well that his great-grandfather dug—a deep shaft about three feet across and lined with bricks. Leaning over the rim, TJ can make out a faint glimmer of water thirty feet below. His grandfather tells him how they used to pull water up with a bucket, but just this

A visit by Americans is a big deal in the small community, and village kids crowd outside the farmhouse window to get a peek at the strangers.

No microwaves or stoves in this house. TJ helps his aunt cook dinner over wood fires.

There is no running water in the house.
TJ's grandfather shows him how to get
water from the well.

Taking a shower on the farm means dumping a bucket of water over your head. TJ helps his younger cousin steady the bucket.

year they added an electric pump and a hose. *Nog* is proud of the pump. It's the only electric machine on the farm, and it makes life much easier. Nevertheless, he wants to show TJ how they drew water in the old days. He throws a bucket down; there is a deep splash; then he pulls it up by a rope, hand over hand. It seems like a lot of work for a bit of water to wash your hands in.

As the day ends, TJ spies the nose and warm brown eyes of an ox peering out of a small thatch barn. But it's time for his family to return to the hotel where they're staying, so he'll have to wait till tomorrow to discover the mysteries of the farm.

4 ➤

Rice Paddies and Water Buffalo

The next morning, TJ can't wait to explore the farm and neighborhood. Only a few acres, the farm would be considered small in America. But not in Vietnam. It's the perfect size for TJ, and every few yards he discovers something new. In the fields grow rice, soybeans, corn, and mulberry leaves to feed silkworms. There is a vegetable garden in front of the house. Lining the footpaths, trees grow coconuts, guavas, papayas, avocados, bananas, and

TJ and his grandfather walk through a mulberry patch, which is grown to feed the farm's silkworms.

Although harmless, the big silkworms are a little too creepy for TJ.

The silkworms grow fat on big trays covered with mulberry leaves, their food. Each worm spins a silk cocoon, which is collected and turned into clothing and fabric used throughout the world.

TJ finds a fruit almost as big as he is growing on a nearby tree.
The jackfruit has a spiny skin but is sweet like a pineapple on the inside.

mangoes. Bamboo and eucalyptus provide wood and shade. The biggest trees have strange green fruits that grow right out of their trunks. Bigger than footballs and covered with spiny knobs, they are called jackfruit. They don't look very appetizing, but the insides are yellow and sweet. Now TJ knows why he hasn't seen any supermarkets; everyone has a supermarket right in their backyard.

One thing TJ is learning about Vietnam: It's a hot place, and May is the hottest time of year. Every day, the temperature rises to nearly 100 degrees. People work in the morning when it's cool and rest in the shade at midday. At home, TJ's mom would turn on the air conditioner. Here, people use old-fashioned ways to keep cool. His grandfather lies on a bamboo bed beneath a shady guava tree. The chickens climb into the rafters of the barn. TJ prefers the hammock. By pushing off the wall with one foot, he can keep the air circulating as if he's in a rocking bed under a fan.

When it cools in late afternoon, people start moving again. Women wearing straw hats work in the rice paddies, and Uncle Thao grabs TJ for a walk along the dirt road. TJ is eager to go. He likes Thao, maybe because his goofy joking reminds him of Uncle Jason, Thao's older brother. Thao looks like Jason and even laughs like Jason. At supper yesterday, Thao reached over to TJ's plate, snatched a whole rice cake, and ate it in one bite with a big grin—just like Jason showing off to TJ.

On the road, people pass them on bicycles carrying loads TJ would never see in Denver. One bicycle carries a pig as big as the bike in a basket. Another comes by with about 100 quacking ducks tied upside down by their feet to a big wooden frame. Down the road, a water buffalo has had the equivalent of a flat tire. One

TJ escapes the midday heat in the farmhouse hammock. By swinging he can cool himself off.

Fixing a flat on a water buffalo is a lot more work than changing a tire. TJ watches as neighboring farmers repair the buffalo's damaged shoe.

The water buffalo is Vietnam's hardest working farm animal. After the buffalo's shoe is repaired, TJ climbs aboard.

shoe has worn out, and three men are nailing on a new one. They are metal like horseshoes except that because a buffalo has split hooves he needs two shoes for each foot. When the men finish, the big animal lumbers into the irrigation ditch and lies in the water with only his head showing. Naturally, a water buffalo's favorite place is in the water.

Although his neighbors use buffalo instead of tractors, Thao is proud of his family's oxen, which are more valuable than buffalo and easier to command. TJ loves these gentle animals and is thrilled when Thao asks him to help plow a new cornfield. From the barn, Thao brings the oxen, the yoke, and the plow, and they head for the field. The oxen follow like dogs, as if they know what to do. At the field, they even stand together, making it easy for Thao to hitch up the plow.

Then, as simple as starting a car, Thao says one word and off they go around the edge of the field. It looks so easy, Thao just

TJ's favorite farm animals are the oxen, which live in a little barn next to the house.

TJ learns how to plow a new field with the oxen.

walking along, occasionally tapping one of the oxen with a bamboo switch to give directions, the plow digging straight, deep grooves. TJ wants to try but sees right away that even though the oxen are doing all the pulling, it's hard work at the back end, too. He tries to keep the plow upright, and angled so it cuts to the right depth. But it's heavy, and TJ falls sideways into the dirt while the oxen keep pulling. After making two passes, TJ turns around. His furrows look like snakes next to Thao's straight lines. He glances at Thao, and his uncle is laughing.

TJ tries another job with his aunt Phieu, helping her in the rice paddy. At this time of year, the rice plants are only a foot high, and the main job is to pull weeds. Because rice needs lots of water, the paddy is flooded. TJ steps barefoot into squishy mud, careful to put his feet between the stalks so he won't crush any of the delicate plants. Phieu shows him how to tell weeds from rice, and

Uncle Thao has a good laugh as TJ attempts to stay aboard one of the oxen.

TJ tries to tell the difference between a weed and a rice plant
as he helps his aunt weed the rice field.

once he starts pulling, weeds are everywhere. It's hard work, bending over in the hot sun with only a bamboo hat for shade. At home, TJ's main chore is to keep his room clean, a job that looks pretty good to him right now.

TJ is dying of thirst after all this hot work. At home he could open the refrigerator and grab a soda. But here you have to harvest your drink. *Nog* hands TJ a special stick and takes him to a coconut tree in the front yard. Using the stick, TJ knocks down one of the heavy green coconuts, ducking so it doesn't land on his head. Then Uncle Thao cuts it open with a big knife and pours the sweet, clear coconut milk into a glass. TJ's not used to seeing water come out of a fruit, and although it tastes pretty good, he'd really rather have a Coke.

Wandering back to the ox barn, TJ spots a bamboo canoe in the rafters. "Uncle Thao," he yells. "Can we take it to the river?" The canoe is not usually used for fun. Its main purpose is to carry farm produce down the river to sell in town. But Thao can't pass up a chance to show off to TJ. With TJ's help, he carries the boat down to the water, where he drops it in with a splash.

Getting coconuts from the palm tree is a tough job. TJ uses a long bamboo stick to shake the coconuts loose.

TJ and his uncle Thao head for the river with the family's bamboo canoe.

Uncle Thao and TJ explore the river that flows by the farm.

The river is perfect for learning to canoe. Thao and TJ paddle past farm fields and under big overhanging trees. A neighboring farmer walks along the bank with a herd of ducks. Around the bend they drift past two boys washing their oxen, and later a man crosses the river in a cart pulled by two water buffalo. The river hasn't changed since TJ's grandfather was a boy. It's a quiet place with no motors and nothing moving faster than a drifting canoe.

While canoeing up the river, TJ and Thao pass farm boys washing their oxen.

As they paddle back to the landing, TJ's four girl cousins are waiting with mischief written all over their faces. "Oh no!" he says, with a big smile. The water is so shallow the girls can walk out to the canoe, and without warning, they start a water fight. In seconds TJ is soaked. Thao jumps out laughing and leaves him to his cousins' mercy. Before long they are all in the river together, splashing and laughing. Cousins are the same everywhere.

Time to abandon ship as TJ's cousins playfully attack the canoe.

Epilogue

In a short time TJ has explored every corner of the farm, but he's sad to leave his new family so soon. He looks forward to seeing his dad and brothers again, but he'll miss his grandparents and the farm, and especially Thao, his newfound uncle. As they

TJ gives his uncle Thao a warm good-bye hug. He'll miss his new uncle very much.